RANDOM ACTS OF KINDNESS

DANNY WALLACE

www.Join-Me.co.uk
EDINBURGH
Kilted
Karma
Army
JOIN ME
Mini
Karma
Army

Mini
Karma
Army
JOIN
ME
Team 2
Hello
stranger!
Join me!
Hello
stranger!
Join me!

Published in 2004 by Ebury Press, an imprint of Ebury Publishing

A Random House Group Company

The Random House Group Limited Reg. No. 954009

Addresses for companies within the Random House Group can be found at www.randomhouse.co.uk

A CIP catalogue record for this book is available from the British Library

The Random House Group Limited supports The Forest Stewardship Council (FSC®), the leading international forest certification organisation. Our books carrying the FSC label are printed on FSC® certified paper. FSC is the only forest certification scheme endorsed by the leading environmental organisations, including Greenpeace. Our paper procurement policy can be found at www.randomhouse.co.uk/environment

Printed and bound by CPI Group (UK) Ltd, Croydon , CR0 4YY

ISBN 9780091901752

Photo credits: Wayne Marshall-Page, Danny Wallace and The Karma Army (thanks!)

Hey!

Kids! Please make sure you tell an adult if you're intending to do a random act of kindness. Don't approach strangers on your own – always make sure someone knows where you are and what you're doing. And anyway, sometimes it's more fun if you do it with your mates!

This book is dedicated to Keith Mitchell.

WELCOME TO KARMAGEDDON

Hello there.

My name's Danny, and I'm a cult leader.

Well, kind of. It all sort of happened by accident... but that's another story, for another book.

What you need to know is this: my cult is a nice cult. A friendly cult. It's not a cult that does much space travel, or believes that humans are actually lizards, or has much chanting. And it's a cult that certainly frowns upon mass suicides.

No. It's a cult called the Karma Army, and it's a cult with a simple message – undertake a random act of kindness for a stranger when you can.

The people who have joined my cult have been performing these random acts for some time now, and have found that it not only benefits other people's lives – but their own, too. And this small book will tell you how.

It's packed with ideas that some of my 8000 followers have road tested for you… from giving a helium balloon to a policeman, to planting a flower in a stranger's garden, to simply making someone feel good about themselves.

We've found that doing something nice for a complete stranger makes *us* feel good. And the fact that there are thousands of other people doing it provides us with the 'excuse' we sometimes need to… well… to just be nice.

Now clearly, a true random act of kindness should be… you know… random. But we hope this little book will at least inspire you to think of your own. And if it doesn't, or you're lazy… well… just copy one of the ones in here. At random.

So read the following couple of hundred pages, and bask in the knowledge that with things like this going on, in real life, every day, maybe the world isn't such a bad place after all…

And you have the power to make it even nicer.

Bye!

'NO ACT OF KINDNESS, HOWEVER SMALL, IS EVER WASTED' - Aesop

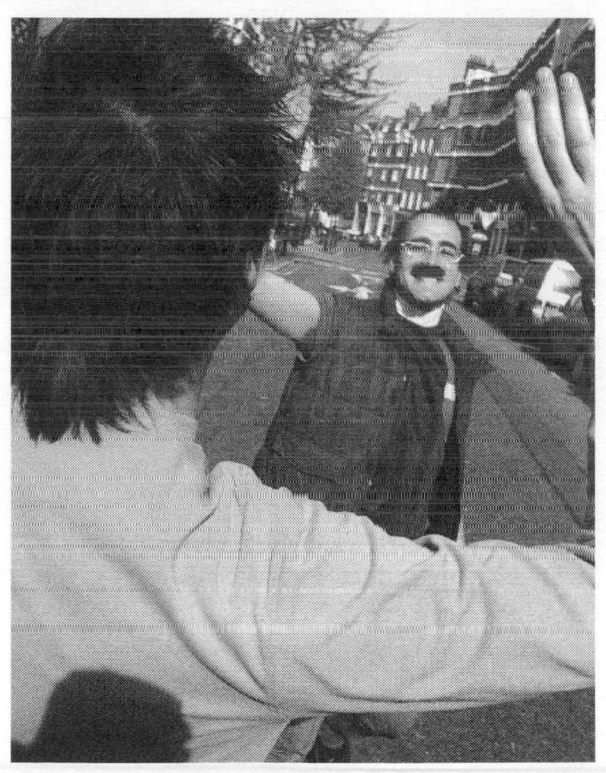

RAOK No. 1

Bellow a cheery hello at a vicar or nun.

Send your compliments to the chef.

Give a slice of your pizza to the delivery man.

Be unfailingly polite to every single person you meet.

Buy a packet of cigars, and leave it behind the reception desk of a maternity ward for all the new fathers.

Phone someone at a call centre and tell them they're doing a good job.

Strike up a conversation with an old man on a bench.

Do a chore at work that someone else usually has to do.

Invite someone new to the pub with your mates.

Give a dog a bone.

Wash your neighbour's car. Whether they like it or not.

Give a stranger a note telling them your mate fancies them.

Buy a pensioner an ice cream.

Hug someone you don't normally hug. Extra points if it's a stranger.

Swap places with the person behind you in the queue.

RAOK No. 16

Teach some policemen to skip.

PROVIDE ENTERTAINMENT!

I was in the pub one afternoon and noticed a group of old men sitting around a table in the corner. They seemed to be having a nice time, swapping stories and sipping at their pints. But I thought they could have a nicer time. So I popped out, bought a pack of cards, and gave them to the old fellas. When I came back two hours later they were still playing, and having loads of fun. They bought me a pint as a thank you! I felt like I'd made a load of old mates!

Rob Thomas, Swansea

Write a letter to the letters page of your local newspaper telling everyone they're great.

Find old scarves and gloves you don't need any more and, on a cold day, offer them to strangers in the street.

Today, give blood. Seriously. Do it.

Look at www.blood.co.uk

Send a postcard to someone you hardly know.

Write to an old teacher, and say thanks.

PICK · ON · YOUR MATES — NICELY!

Me and a few mates were bored one night and came up with an ace plan... to pick on another friend, but with kindness...

We thought it'd be funny to bewilder him with kindness, and for the next few days he was incredibly confused as he received a voucher for a free meal for two at his local restaurant, a free pint (which we'd secretly arranged with the landlord of his local pub), and a load of free cat food for his (admittedly ugly) cat.

We now create one piece of 'luck' for him every week... and he still doesn't know who's doing it...!

ANONYMOUS, BIRMINGHAM

If you're driving, let someone in ahead of you.

If you see an old person struggling in a supermarket, help them do their shopping.

Feed the ducks.

Send a valentine card to the ugliest person you know.

Say something nice about someone behind their back.

At a sports day, cheer for someone you blatantly don't know.

Find the most obscure charity you can – one that probably makes about a fiver a year – and donate a few quid.

Forgive someone.

Give your old watch to someone who doesn't have one.

Listen to somcone's problem without immediately comparing it to one of your own.

Find the number of the person who sent you some (unwanted) spam e-mail, and phone them to say thanks.

USE · COUPONS!

I received some coupons for a certain type of 'lady-product' that I clearly had no use for… but instead of throwing the coupons out, I left them next to the appropriate lady-product in the supermarket. Thanks to me, some lady got two lady-products for the price of one! Which could certainly have helped her in any sort of lady-emergency that may have happened afterwards!

DAMIEN LOWE, DUNDEE

NB This coupon kindness is not limited to lady-products. It can also be used with coupons for biscuits, say, or even washing powder – although that's more boring.

Give water to people as they leave a gym.

Assist a policeman in his duties.

Plant a flower in someone's garden, under cover of darkness.

Buy a scratchcard and hand it to a stranger.

Buy an unpopular CD single.

If you can't make it to a gig – don't waste the ticket. Give it to a stranger.

RAOK No. 42

Offer some handy advice to a tourist.

Give a kite to a father and son in the park.

Hide a complimentary note in a book in the library.

Choose a local shop instead of a supermarket. (Unless you are a shoplifter.)

BUY · AN · OLD · LADY A · HAT!

I was in a charity shop, looking at some dodgy old records, when I noticed an old lady trying on a hat. She seemed to love it, and looked at herself in the mirror and smiled. From the conversation she was having with the lady behind the counter it became clear that she'd been in the shop to see it a couple of times before but just couldn't afford it. When she left, I had a look at the price tag and saw that it was only a couple of quid. So I bought it (explaining to the woman behind the counter why!) and ran down the road after her. I thought she was going to cry when I handed it over. It was great.

ANNA JESSOP, SWANSEA

OFFER · AN UNSOLICITED · PINT!

Me and my boyfriend spotted a Chinese couple who were just finishing their drinks... They were about to get another round in, but we beat them to it! They were rather surprised... but happy!

KATE, LEAMINGTON SPA

Give someone the benefit of the doubt.

Get someone who looks cold a hot chocolate. Everybody loves a hot chocolate! Especially cold people, like Christmas shoppers, or an Eskimo.

Smile at everyone you see.

Compliment someone on their choice of footwear (even if it's rubbish).

Pay for the coffee of the person behind you in the queue.

Drop some flowers off at a nursing home.

On a rainy day, hand a spare umbrella to someone at a bus stop.

Stand outside a hairdressers, and tell whoever walks out that they look lovely.

Stand at a doorway for ten minutes, and hold it open for whoever walks through.

Give an apple to a bored security guard.

Leave 20p in a phonebox.

If someone stops you and asks you to take part in a survey, fight your instincts. Do the survey as best you can.

Run ahead of a street cleaner and pick up some rubbish for them.

WIN SOMETHING FOR SOMEONE!

Enter someone else's name into a competition. I did it and my neighbour won a mug!

PAUL JACOBS, CARDIFF

Loads of the big chain coffee shops are willing to give away free coffee at the end of the night instead of wasting the left-over coffee. With a flask, someone who needs it can have a warm drink at hand all night.

MATT WHITBY, NEWBURY

Give your newspaper to a cab driver.

Wish an astronaut good luck.

Write to: An Astronaut,
NASA Headquarters, 300 E St. SW,
Washington DC, USA.

Leave a nice note for the cleaners at work.

RAOK No. 66

Top up a parking meter that's about to run out.

Compliment your bus driver on his or her skills as you leave the bus.

Write a postcard for whoever works in the post room at your place of work, telling them what a sterling job they're doing.

If you're returning a video, rewind it first.

Find some old books you don't want any more, and leave them on your bus, train or plane. (Make sure the books aren't about bus, train or plane crashes, though.)

Pick up some teas and biscuits for the people you work with.

Give someone a shoulder massage. (Make sure that they want one first, otherwise you could be done for harassment.)

MAKE · UP · FOR · SOMEONE ELSE'S · BAD · DEED!

I was walking past a bus stop recently and saw an old lady trying her best to make it to the stop before the bus moved off. To be honest, I'm fairly sure that the driver saw her approaching but he decided to leave anyway, pretty much at the last moment. When the lady saw she had missed her bus she looked incredibly sad; so much so that I hailed a cab and gave the driver a tenner, telling him to take her wherever she needed to go. She couldn't believe it. I felt amazing.

JOANNE, GLASGOW

Share your umbrella with someone during a downpour.

On a frosty morning, scrape the ice off the windscreen of the car next to yours. If you don't have a car, just do this for anyone at random.

Pat a dog.

Unless your waiter or waitress was utterly rubbish, say something really nice about them to someone who looks more senior than them as you leave the restaurant.

Let someone keep the change.

Erect a bird feeder.

If someone cuts you up in traffic, instead of flicking them the finger, smile and wave at them like a lunatic.

In thc canteen, offer to take someone else's tray back with yours.

Create a 'Free Box'... Put some stuff you no longer want or need in a box, write 'Free' on it, and leave it next to a bench somewhere.

SHARE YOUR MEAL!

If you can't finish your meal at a restaurant, pop the rest in a box and hand it to someone who needs it. I did, and it was a lovely feeling.

ELLA, CHESTER

HELP FOREIGN SCHOOLKIDS LEARN ENGLISH!

Whenever I've finished a book or a load of magazines, I send 'em to a load of kids in the Chinese countryside who are desperate to learn English.

DAMI NEWMAN, COVENTRY

NB You can send stuff to random Chinese kids too! Send them to: The English Students, LingLing Xue Yuan, Yongzhou, Hunan, 425000, China.

Sign a petition.

How? Go to www.amnesty.org

When you're in a hotel and you get one of those 'How was the service?' cards, fill it out. Try and remember one of the staff's name and praise them to the heavens.

Tidy up the shopping trolleys at the supermarket.

At the traffic lights, smile at the person in the car next to yours.

Put a pound coin where someone will find it.

RAOK No. 90

Tell someone your very best joke. (Keep it clean and avoid racism or anything about dwarves.)

Give a pregnant woman a foot rub.

On a Sunday morning, pop round to a hungover friend's house, bringing with you bacon, eggs, beans and toast… Make them a fry-up and a cup of tea.

Lay some flowers at an otherwise bare grave.

Give someone an apple.

If a friend of yours is going far away, send a fax to their hotel, just to say hello.

TREAT · A · CABBIE!

Hail a cab, and when the driver winds his window down, give him a packet of peanuts. That's what me and my mates do sometimes, and it never fails to please.

EMMA THOMAS, SWINDON

DO · SOMETHING FOR · FREE!

I'm a mechanic, and, once a week, I give a free oil change to whoever needs one. Fair enough, in the early days I only did it for fit women, but nowadays, it's anyone's!

DANIEL ANDERSON, BANBURY

Laugh at someone's story. Even if it is quite frankly terrible.

Pay for someone's shoe shine.

At the pub, buy the table next to yours a packet of crisps to share.

Be someone's biggest fan.

Give a disposable camera to a group of people you see having fun.

If you like someone, make sure they know.

Make a stranger laugh.

RAOK No. 105

Choose a friend and organise a night in the pub in their honour. Keep it a secret and have T-shirts printed with their face on it, as well as a small banner with their name on. Do it completely at random, and make sure they don't buy a drink all evening. They will be utterly confused but very, very happy. Make sure there's more than just the two of you there, though, else you'll look a bit odd in your T-shirts.

Give a kid a set of coloured pencils or crayons. Or better still, a box of chalk, because then at least when they write something rude on your trousers you can brush it off.

Lend an ear.

Pull some weeds from someone's front garden. (Make sure you know the difference between a weed and a flower, though.)

Leave a saucer of milk out for a cat or a dog.

TIDY · UP · FOR THE · CLEANER!

One night everyone in my office decided to treat the cleaner... so we finished work twenty minutes early and set about cleaning the whole office up... When she arrived at six o'clock she was stunned... especially when she saw the tea and cakes we'd brought in for her. We all sat about for half an hour and had a great time. Then we all went home and left her to tidy up the tea and cakes.

Sara Owen, Leeds

Buy free-range stuff.

Let someone beat you at arm-wrestling.

If you've taken a picture of a particularly fantastic night out, make a copy for everyone who was there.

Hide a surprise under someone's pillow. (Horses' heads are discouraged.)

Make someone feel important.

Install a smoke detector in a lazy friend's house.

Post a packet of seeds through the letterbox of someone with a particularly nice garden.

Vote for the good guys.

Smile for the speed camera.

Give a random pregnant woman something for the baby (not cigarettes or wine).

Buy a packet of crisps from the vending machine but leave them in there.

CONGRATULATE A·STRANGER!

I was walking down my street the other day when I noticed that there was a banner on someone's front door saying 'BABY BOY'. It appeared they'd just had a child. So I popped off, bought some flowers, and left them on the strangers doorstep. The next day when I walked past, I saw that they'd put them up in the window, which made me smile all day...

KNELLER, LONDON

Write a cheery 'hello' on a banknote and then spend it.

Play knock down ginger, but leave a little gift for the confused door-answering resident.

Hand the man who works in the shed at the car park a packet of wine gums.

Give a tramp a harmonica.

Say ‘bless you’ when someone sneezes.

Start a standing ovation at a school play, or panto, or karaoke night, or anywhere else at all. Make sure you do it at the end of the performance, though, rather than halfway through. Actors can be touchy.

RAOK No. 130

Help a bellboy.

Make someone their own personal compilation tape.

Donate your knackered old car to charity.

Make sure someone doesn't skip breakfast.

BUY · A · TUB · OF COLESLAW · FOR · A PORTUGUESE · MAN CALLED · RUI!

I bought a tub of coleslaw for a Portuguese man called Rui. He was trying to sell me dodgy travelcards for the London Underground at the time. We got chatting, he was lovely, and I handed over the coleslaw. It was a small and somehow pointless gesture, but it was all I had, and he seemed to really appreciate it. And sometimes the smallest and most pointless gestures can mean the most, I guess.

John Foster, Surbiton

If you've got a Polaroid camera, take a picture of a tourist looking touristy and then give it to them, free.

Share your lunch with someone.

Give a kid your battered old football.

FOR THE LADIES

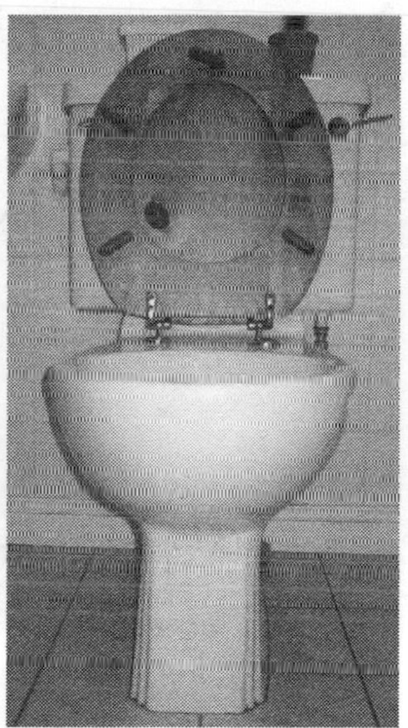

FOR THE GENTS

RAOK No. 138

If you're a fella, put the toilet seat down.
If you're a lady, pop it up.

Buy a copy of the *Big Issue*, and then give it back to the seller.

Send a nice text message to someone you never text.

Plant a flower in someone else's allotment.

Old men with pipes are brilliant. To encourage this welcome sight more in society, the next time you see an old man carrying a pipe, pop off to the newsagent to buy him some extra tobacco.

Stroke a cat.

At a football match, buy more teas than you need and hand them out.

Write a nice note for the postman on the back of an envelope you're about to send.

BE · NICE · TO AMBULANCE · DRIVERS!

I once dropped by an emergency ward on my way home from the pub, and left a selection of snacks I'd bought from the late-night garage. I told the woman on reception to give them to the night-shift workers. She told me ambulance drivers tend to like Pringles, so that was nice.

JAMES BENNETT, MANCHESTER

GIVE · A · BOOK!

If I'm feeling particularly generous, I like to hide book tokens in random books in the bookshop… It's great to think that someone will pick up a book, take it to the counter, buy it, but then eventually get it for free. It's especially good to hide them in books about parenting, or exam revision books…

LAURA MATTHEWS, YORK

Wrap a pound coin in aluminium foil and give it to one of those street artists who dress up all in silver and stand very still – it will show them you appreciate their art. (You can laugh about it with your friends later.)

In the pub, get your mates to contribute a quid and then sponsor a child in Africa. Every month do the same. Get everyone to write a note to the kid and then send them off. The notes, I mean, not your mates. Don't go sending your mates to Africa.

Dress up as a wizard for a mate who's reading Harry Potter.

Give a CD or tape to someone about to embark on a long car journey.

Buy popcorn for a stranger at the cinema.

RAOK No. 153

Applaud a lady who's clearly made an effort.

Students coming to Britain have it tough. If you've any old mugs, or crockery, or sheets, or duvets, drop them off at your local Student Union. The money they save on all that stuff can be spent on beer and Rizlas, or, at a push, books.

Give someone a lift.

If you know a friend is at home in bed with a cold or the flu, drop a small 'Get Well' parcel around. But remember to keep your distance. Friends don't have to share *everything*.

MAKE · AN · OLD · MAN VERY · HAPPY!

We found this old man in a pub in Brussels... He had just retired that day, and when we found out, we bought him a few drinks, a packet of nuts, and lavished him with female attention! It was lots of fun. Especially for him!

JOAN VANDEN BOSSCHE, BELGIUM

FEED · THE · HOMELESS!

I met a bloke called Jeff the other night in Sydney whose life has changed thanks to a random act of kindness. He was a rich restaurateur who was sitting on a park bench one night when a homeless fella walked up and offered him his only possession: his blanket. The homeless guy thought Jeff must be homeless too... and yet was willing to give away the only thing he owned. It had such an impact on Jeff that he packed in his restaurant and started a non-religious charity that now feeds 500 people a night... That was ten years ago. And what happened to the original homeless guy? He was best man at Jeff's wedding!

LORNA MANN, SYDNEY

NB If you're Australian, check out www.justenoughfaith.org for more!

If you're getting a big order in at McDonald's or Burger King, buy an extra bag of fries, and give them to someone who needs them, outside. Don't forget the ketchup. It's the details that make it special.

Compliment a large woman.

Say ‘have a nice day’ even if you’ve never even been to America.

Offer to swap seats on the bus or train so two friends can sit next to each other.

If someone has food around their mouth, tell them quickly and discreetly. Laugh about it later on your own.

Phone an elderly relative and talk to them for a minimum of ten minutes. Time yourself if need be.

Give old socks
or gloves to a
homeless person.

Take a morning
coffee to a busy
receptionist.

Pretend to take an
interest in someone's
dull story.

Ask someone more questions than you answer.

Help someone take a pram up or down some stairs. As long as it's *their* pram. For God's sake don't start helping people steal prams.

BUY · A · WEDDING GIFT · FOR · A · COUPLE YOU'VE · NEVER · MET!

Lots of wedding lists are now on-line. So why not pick one at random and get the couple a little gift? I've done it twice now… I imagine it feels a little odd opening your wedding gifts and then finding there's one from a complete stranger. But I imagine it feels rather good, too.

GARETH SAUNDERS, EDINBURGH

NB Some celebrities now put their wedding lists on-line too. Gareth recently noticed that the Beverly Hills 90210 *actress Tori Spelling had put hers on the web. He bought her a muffin tray.*

Give an apple to your teacher.

Leave some fresh fruit and vegetables outside a student house. They will probably try and turn it into beer, but at least you tried.

Resist the urge to kill.

Serve your family or loved one breakfast in bed.

Buy an energy-efficient lightbulb.

Help a fly or daddy-long-legs out of your house rather than squash it.

RAOK No. 177

Buy a pizza and hand it out on the street.

Hoist a short person onto your shoulders at a gig.

As a family or flatshare, sponsor one of the rubbish animals at London Zoo. Monkeys get all the money. Pity the Slow Loris.

BUY · SOMEONE · IN INDIA · A · COW!

It provides a family in need with the milk they need to live on, they can sell the rest, and the cow dung can be used to fertilise the fields. And all for less than £200!

These people take all the hassle out of it for you… www.goodgifts.org

You can even name the cow – after a family member, maybe, or an old teacher who resembles a cow in some way, like *my* old teacher, Mrs Udders.

GRETA MCMAHON, LONDON

SPOIL AN AMBASSADOR!

Me and my friend Dan met the Estonian ambassador recently, and, because ambassadors are always spoiling other people, we gave her some Ferrero Rocher. She seemed very pleased, but I think that, as she was Estonian, she may not have got the reference. Still – free chocolates!

RICHARD, LONDON

Ask an old man whether he knows any good war stories. And then listen.

Take your glass back to the bar.

When you've got the builders in, make sure the kettle's on.

Being a lighthouse keeper is a lonely job. Especially if you're in one of the most isolated lighthouses in the world! Write a friendly postcard to:

The Lighthouse Keeper,
South Solitary Lighthouse,
near Coffs Harbour, NSW, Australia.

Water your plants.

Try and boost a bad TV show's ratings.

Tell your dentist you'd like teeth like his.

Give your unused board games to the kid next door.

Let your hairdresser try something new.

Look up some basic First Aid techniques. Think of it as a kindness investment.

If you see a blind person by the traffic lights, don't go silent and pretend you're not there. Ask if they'd like help.

PAY · FOR · A STRANGER'S · MEAL!

Last half term, visiting my local café for my traditional Friday morning bacon and egg sandwich, I noticed a mum and her little boy at a table by the window. She had toast and he was tucking in to a fried breakfast. I thought it would be nice to chip in and pay for their mini feast. The following Friday I learnt that the mum in question had been unceremoniously dumped by her husband, and with ridiculous debts had been rendered homeless prior to finding a one-bed council flat. The visit to the café was the only treat she could afford for her little boy in his half-term holiday and when she found someone had paid anonymously, she burst into tears.

It may sound just a little selfish but I felt really good about that one.

ADRIAN THOMPSON, CHELTENHAM

Phone your parents on your birthday and thank them. (Also, tell them you hope they enjoyed it.)

If you see an incredibly cheap flight, buy it, and offer it to one of your friends.

Give a pot plant to a bus driver. It will brighten up their dashboard.

Stand outside a WeightWatchers meeting and tell people how trim they look.

Support Live Music.

RAOK No. 198

Repair relations with the French.

Meddle with a colleague's screensaver. Put a lovely message on there for them, such as I LOVE YOU AND I ALWAYS WILL. (It is best not to do this if you have a prison record for stalking.)

Don't club seals.

Wish good luck to all you pass outside the local Youth Court.

Turn up outside a stranger's wedding with extra confetti.

Stop Rik Waller.

Let someone keep your lighter.

ABUSE · THE · INTERNAL MAIL · SYSTEM · AT · YOUR PLACE · OF · WORK!

Send a random colleague a chocolate bar through the post. I usually choose names that I enjoy, such as Kim Kong, or Judy Doody.

JOE, LONDON

EMPTY · YOUR · POCKETS OF · LOLLIPOPS!

One day, on impulse, I decided to stick a load of lollipops in my coat jacket. I ended up giving them to shop assistants, and bus drivers, and anyone else who'd done me a service that day. People didn't quite know how to react at first, but they always took one, and they always smiled a huge smile. Made me feel ridiculously good...

TOM WAITE, NUNEATON

Compliment a lesbian couple on their haircuts.

Stand outside a doctor's surgery handing out apples.

Record someone's favourite programme for them.

Give a supplement from your newspaper to someone who needs something to read on the train.

Be the designated driver.

Stay late at a party and help clean up.

RAOK No. 213

Make up an award, and give it to someone in the street. Everybody loves an award!

Help the person next door move out. (Particularly if you're the one who drove them out.)

Help the person next door move in. (Don't mention why the last person moved out.)

Give your ancient videogames console to the kids next door, or to students, who will appreciate the irony value of receiving a Super Nintendo or Megadrive.

If there's a new person in the office, invite them out for a drink with everyone else after work. The next morning they'll feel much more welcome. Plus, if you fancy them – imagine the points you'll score!

Get a group of mates, wrap some random presents, and, on the way home from the pub, hand them to total strangers.

Get an organ donor card. You could save a few lives. And it looks cool in your wallet.

GIVE · SOMEONE · A LOVELY · AFTERNOON!

Recently, I heard about an elderly lady who'd been having a tough time... We'd never met her, but on a whim, we decided to go round to her house en masse... We managed to convince some other people to come with us and ordered a couple of taxis to pick us up. On the way to her house we bought cakes and biscuits and flowers from a random shop, and you should have seen her face when we turned up, out of the blue... We stayed there for about an hour, and chatted lots, and had an incredible time. The weird thing was, the shop we stopped at to buy the stuff turned out to have been the place she'd worked at for 65 years of her life! Odd. But what I learnt that day was that you should never underestimate the effect that a bit of kindness from a bunch of random strangers can bring...

JAMES FROST, HEREFORD

If you see someone sitting on their own during a pub quiz, invite them onto your team.

If your office is planning a Secret Santa and you've got to spend £10... spend £11.

Compliment a gay
man on his choice
of life partner.

Tell a sweaty
woman she has a
healthy glow.

On a sunny day,
give someone a
spare pair of shades.

Tell a twin that you never really liked the other one.

Tell a triplet that the other two are just copying his style.

If you're a boss, send everyone home half an hour early.

RAOK No. 229

Liberate some rubber ducks.
Leave them where kids will find them.

BE · NICE · TO · A TRAFFIC · WARDEN!

I saw quite a grumpy-looking traffic warden walking around the centre of town and decided that as they get a rough time from the public most of the time, I would try and cheer her up. So I bought a helium balloon from a bloke next to the market and wandered up to present it to her. She was so touched! She couldn't take it, however, because apparently it's against regulations for traffic wardens to walk about with helium balloons. So we gave it to a woman pushing a pram, and we all had a good laugh. Hopefully the traffic warden will have been too distracted by the morning's events to have given too many tickets out!

AMANDA LORD, LEICESTER

Ask someone for their autograph.

If you're going to a party, take paper plates and plastic cups, to save your host from washing up afterwards. (Also, it's cheaper than a bottle of wine.)

Tell someone you used to have a crush on them.

Shops like Iceland are forever doing 'Buy One Get One Free' deals. One day, put all the free stuff you get in a separate bag, and hand it to a stranger.

RAOK No. 235

Give a visitor to your town or city a meaningful souvenir.

According to musical folklore, ‘you’ve got to pick a pocket or two’. Remember: you don’t. (Unless you are a pickpocket, or the man who chooses pockets for particular styles of trouser.)

Ask if you can sign a stranger’s plaster cast.

Give a foreign student an international phone card. It'll make Britain seem less lonely.

If you know your neighbour is on holiday, pick up their mail for them. DO NOT STEAM IT OPEN.

During a power cut, offer candles to your neighbours.

If you're picking up the Sunday papers, buy an extra one, and shove it through someone's door.

Help a child with their homework.

A few months ago my friend Fiona was driving over the Erskine Bridge on her way to Glasgow and, as a random act of kindness, decided to pay at the toll booth for the car behind her as well.

The next week I was sitting on a bus, having a chat with the bus driver. I started to tell him about the random nice stuff we've all been doing, when he pipes up with, 'Oh! That happened to me recently! I was driving over the Erskine Bridge when it happened…'

And of course, I knew what had happened next.

So I told him that by complete chance I knew who was responsible. Turned out he'd been on his way to the funeral of a friend, and really felt like someone was looking out for him that day… It was amazing how much it had meant to him.

CRAIG JOHNSTON, EDINBURGH

Take a picture of a loved one – one that looks nice – and then frame it.

Give a lollipop to a lollipop lady.

Keep a Lemsip in your drawer at work in case someone gets a cold.

• **Goodness Me!** You look lovely today! Have you done something with your hair? It suits you!

RAOK No. 247

Place a free small ad telling the reader how lovely they look.

Take some magazines to the dentists, and then leave them there afterwards. This does not apply to pornography.

Clean someone's windscreen at a traffic lights and then run off.

Go and see a play you know is rubbish.

Make an old man very happy – make an old nan sit on his lappy.

Down the pub, toast a random friend at the top of your voice.

Give a flower seller a pound and tell them to hand the next person who passes some flowers.

Hand a twenty pence piece to someone fumbling for change at the station toilets. Time is of the essence!

SPREAD · YOUR WINNINGS!

I won a massive £1 with a scratchcard one day. Usually, I'd have bought another scratchcard but for some reason this day was different. I asked the man to give me my winnings in 20p coins, and then I went outside to the row of phoneboxes opposite the shop. I left 20p on the top of each phone and then went and sat on a bench. It was great seeing people walk in and realise someone had already paid for their call!

TONY HODGES, HEREFORD

COMPENSATE A VICTIM!

I was recently walking by a fruit stall in the East End of London and noticed some little rascal nicking an apple... so I went to a rival fruit stall, bought an apple, and presented it to the first stall holder. He was happy (and confused) and gobbled it straight up.

LAUREN, ALDGATE

I spotted my local MP at a rugby match and approached him immediately. 'Would you like a tube of Smarties?' I said, and it turned out that he did. We had a lovely chat and, after he'd checked the seal quite carefully, he accepted the sweeties with a smile.

GARETH SAUNDERS, EDINBURGH

Leave a pot of jam outside a stranger's door just before breakfast.

Wave at a baby.

Tie an elderly person's loose shoelace. (Resist the urge to tie them together.)

Offer a tissue to a snotty commuter.

Tell a man with a beard he looks wise and enigmatic, even if he actually looks like a tramp.

Plant a tree.

How? Ridiculously easily. Go to www.futureforests.com

RAOK No. 264

Buy a chocolate and then give it to the man who sold it to you.

Pay for an extra game at the bowling alley for some strangers.

Hold the lift for someone, even if they're miles away.

Buy a six-pack and give two away.

Scrub a gnome.

Make an extra sandwich and give it someone at random.

Offer to take photos at a special event.

Phone your local radio station and ask them to dedicate a song to someone you know is listening.

STOP · THE · BAGPIPES!

As a random act of kindness, I wander around Edinburgh giving bottles of cheap wine to the bagpipers you get on almost every street corner. Not only does it make the piper very happy, but it also gives us locals a rest from the constant wailing.

WORM, EDINBURGH

HELP · PEOPLE · ENJOY A · BAD · FILM!

Me and my friend were off to see a quite appallingly bad film recently, but we got there early. Rather than just sit there, we disappeared off to buy a huge bag of Starbursts, and then put one on every seat we could. It was fantastic to watch people come in, take a seat, take a sweet, and start to watch the film with a smile on their face. It didn't last, though. As I said, it was quite appallingly bad.

JOANNA MORRIS, ABERDEEN

One morning I got up ridiculously early and washed my neighbours' cars. I then went back to bed. I think I may still have been a bit drunk from the night before, to be honest.

TOM BEASLEY, NOTTINGHAM

Re-record your answerphone message to include a random compliment. 'Have you been working out?' and 'I like those shoes – are they new?' are usually winners.

Take someone's dog for a walk.

Text someone goodnight.

Hug your mum for no reason whatsoever.

Keep your complimentary bag of aeroplane peanuts and give them to a stranger.

PEANUTS MAKE A TASTY TREAT – WHATEVER THE WEATHER!

I used to be under the impression that in Britain it was illegal to talk to someone else while sitting on a train, but one day someone started talking to me. We chatted for a while, and eventually got onto the subject of the lady's grandfather, who apparently liked peanuts. Feeling a little cheeky and in the mood for a random act of kindness, I persuaded the lady to give me her grandad's address. She did, and when I got off the train I e-mailed loads of people whose addresses I had on me. And over the course of the next three or four days, that old man received, anonymously, in the post, from all over the UK, about 80 packets of peanuts. I hope it made his day, because it certainly made mine.

DW, LONDON

Give someone a complimentary nickname, like 'lovelycheeks' or 'shiny-shins'.

Leave a bowl of milk out in the garden for a hedgehog, or, if you're reading this in Africa, a lion.

Make someone's day.

Give up your seat for someone on the bus.

Give a bored security guard your newspaper. It will distract him while you rob the place. (Only joking.)

On the way home from the pub with your mates, stop at an all-night garage and buy a loaf of bread and some bacon, and give it to a passer-by for their breakfast.

Tidy the office kitchen.

RAOK No. 287

Ensure someone eats the recommended five pieces of fruit or vegetables a day.

Start a conversation with a stranger at a bus stop. Unless you are the bus driver, in which case it's probably best to just keep on moving and save the conversations for your own time.

Phone your gran.

Drop a bottle of unwanted sherry off at an old people's home.

Offer to clean your colleague's mouse. The computer kind, clearly.

Vacuum a communal hallway.

HUG · AN ESTATE · AGENT!

One afternoon, we piled into a local estate agent, and hugged one! It was lovely!

MISS HALLIFAX, KENT

Tell a customer service adviser you enjoyed their choice of holding music.

On a rainy day, offer a tissue to a specky bloke so he can wipe his glasses.

Foil a robbery.

Often, Buddhist monks rely on donations of food. Give a monk a Mars bar.

Leave your pound in the shopping trolley.

On a hot day, share your sunscreen.

On a bus, train or plane, offer a fellow passenger a mint.

Go to google.com and search under 'Free Samples'. Order as many free samples as you can, and then hand them out at random!

Share a handy tip.

Don't wear fur.

Volunteer for an hour a week, minutes from your home.

How? Go to www.do-it.org.uk

Pay for someone's laundry.

OFFER SOMEONE A LIFT

I'd just finished my weekly shop and was heading for my car when I saw the most incredibly frail old woman carrying a small bag of shopping, walking so slowly away. I just had the urge to help her, so I asked her if she'd like a lift home. She said yes immediately and was hugely grateful... It turned out that her carer had become ill and hadn't been to see her in ten days... She'd run out of food and the only reason that she'd gone to the shops on her own was that she'd have starved otherwise. It felt good to help a complete stranger who as it turned out was in dire need of help but would never have asked for it. I gave her my number in case she ever needs help again.

BENEDICT, LIVERPOOL

Recycle.

Give the man who has to sit in the box at the top of a crane all day a tiny, cheap radio to listen to.

Offer your aeroplane window seat to someone who'd prefer it.

Pay for a stressed friend's massage. (The proper kind, mind you. Steer clear of Soho.)

Phone a random foreign number and congratulate them on a past sporting victory.

RAOK No. 312

Organise a mass rally and give out presents to complete and utter strangers.

If you get your shopping delivered, order an extra bottle of water or a banana and then give it to the person who's had to lug it all the way to your front door.

Lend some videos to an ill pal.

Single-handedly stop world hunger.

How? Go to www.thehungersite.com – your quick clicks mean free food fast.

Buy some onion rings for the car behind you at the Drive-Thru.

Buy someone a 'lucky pen' for their exam.

HELP · A · BORED TOILET · MAN!

There's this bloke whose job it is to sit on a chair in the toilets of my local club making sure no one nicks the soap or draws on the walls. He sits there for hours and hours on end, and never says a word. So one night me and my mates brought him a pint, a packet of crisps, and a magazine we had found about gardening. He was thrilled and now he chats to us whenever we're in there, which, although lovely, can also be a little distracting when you're trying to take aim.

Richard Fenton-Smith, Greenwich

Hold up a sign that says 'Free Good Deeds' and see what happens.

Give an elderly person a lift to the shops.

Bring a friend's pet a treat.

Telemarketers have it tough. Next time one rings you, heartily wish them good luck.

Phone Stevie Wonder and tell him you just called to say you love him, too.

Polish a hearse.

RAOK No. 325

Invite the clergy round for a Sunday roast.

Take your parents back to the place they first met. (Unless they are divorced or still live there.)

Visit the website of Gary and Marilyn Deeds, who retired in 1990.

Go to www.thegooddeeds.com

If you're writing someone a letter, enclose a stamp for their reply.

Play Trivial Pursuit and let a thick friend win.

Learn how to use a toilet brush.

MAKE SOMEONE'S BIRTHDAY!

Some friends and us were having a picnic in Regents Park one sunny afternoon, when we spotted an old woman on the other side of the lake who had a Happy Birthday balloon tied to her chair. So we jumped into some boats, rowed across the lake, and seventeen of us serenaded her with a beautiful rendition of Happy Birthday. She seemed to be incredibly pleased...

SCOTTY & RUFOUS, LONDON

Turn your Walkman down on the train.

Pick a random name and address from the phonebook and every once in a while send them an amusing postcard, detailing your thoughts and philosophies on life.

Those charity muggers you see on the high street spend all day being ignored. Buy one a coffee and then run off.

Tell a Norwegian to stop whaling. Word will soon get round.

Send a present to your postman.

Pump up someone's bicycle tyres.

Whistle while you work. Unless asked not to.

Pop a sugar cube next to an ants' nest.

Take some toys to a maternity ward and tell them to give them to whoever needs them.

Give a big man a small cactus.

Leave a small tip out in an envelope marked 'Paper-boy'.

GIVE · SOMEONE A · CARD!

This was the first random act of kindness I ever consciously did... I was feeling shy about it so I decided I'd do something which I could quickly walk away from. So I bought a greetings card and stuck a fiver in it. Eventually I plucked up the courage to give it to the bloke behind the counter in the sweet shop. He was surprised and delighted... and I felt absolutely great. It was honestly one of the best feelings I've ever had, even though it was from something so small.

TOM ANDERSON, AINSDALE

RAoK 27 Feb 2004

Write some sincere fanmail to a pop star who probably doesn't get any.

Wave hello to the incredibly bored security guard watching the CCTV monitors.

Scoop-a-poop.

RAOK No. 347

Contradict demeaning graffiti.

Fax your MP with a useful suggestion or a handy hint.

It's easy! Go to www.faxyourmp.com and they'll take care of it!

Help an old man across the road.

Listen to a story without once interrupting.

Write a funny postcard to a random Canadian soldier!

Send it to: Any Canadian Soldier, *OP HALO* (5104), PO Box. 5104 Stn Forces, Belleville ON K8N 5W6, Canada.

If you're at school, get your cookery class to bake a load of cakes and then hand them out at lunchtime.

TREAT · A · STRANGER TO · A · FILM!

My friend Steff decided, as a large-scale random act of kindness, to hire the local cinema for the afternoon. It only cost £150, and could seat about 100 people. The manager didn't really understand why Steff wanted to hire it for a bunch of complete strangers, but agreed anyway. Steff spent the day flyering local charities and schools to tell them he'd pay for them to go to the pictures, and in the end the manager was so touched by the kindness on offer he gave everyone their drinks and snacks for free! Just shows how kindness spreads like a strange little rash... but a rash you wouldn't mind getting. So long as it wasn't on your face.

PAUL, CHESTER

Hand cups of tca to outdoor workmen.

Start a word-of-mouth campaign to help an ailing shop or takeaway.

Hide 50p down the back of someone's sofa.

Enclose a stick of chewing gum when paying your bills by post. Make sure it is unused.

Take advantage of 3-for-2 book deals – but give the free one away to someone outside the shop.

Sandwich shop chains often chuck out their unsold sandwiches at the end of the night – convince one to give you a load, and then hand 'em out to late-night travellers or people who look hungry.

Come up with a detailed strategy to bring about world peace.

In a restaurant, anonymously pay for a random table's starter.

Let a fat man win a race.

RAOK No. 362

Stop the mugging. Start the hugging.

On a hot day, give a cat or dog a small bowl of vanilla ice cream.

REWARD SOMEONE ELSE'S NICENESS!

The other day, I woke up late for work. I realised if I got the bus I'd be incredibly late so I ordered a taxi. But on the way I realised I only had a fiver on me... and the fare was £8... The driver just said, 'Look, call it a fiver then...' It was so lovely of him, and as a thank you I tracked him down later and gave him a KitKat. So we were both winners!

SIOBHAN, FIFE

RAOK No. 365

Hand this book to a stranger when you've finished with it!

Write your name here ___________ and pass it on!

If you received this book as a random act of kindness from a stranger, write your name below and then hand it on to another stranger!

____

____

____

____

____

____

____

____

THANKS TO...

Greta McMahon, Jonesy and Cobbett, Wag, Jon Bond, Katie, Jen, Brol, Jake Lingwood, Simon Trewin, Stina Smemo, Diana Riley, Dave @ Two Associates, Dominican Joly, Richard Webb, Al (who taught policemen to skip), Alistair Griffin, and each and every member of the Karma Army, and everyone who contributed an idea... including (but not only)... Gareth Saunders, Tom Anderson, Joan Vanden Bossche, Claire Mimnagh, Laura Mack, Gaz Haman, Matt Whitby, Richard Fenton-Smith, Jason Smith, Steff Worthington, Damien Benner, Tony Hodges, James Frost, Douglas Gresham, Chris Knight, Warren Bonathan, John West, all the various Hazels, Simon Brake, Dawn Shepherd, Lu Gardner, Alex Whittam, Simon Bishop, Annie Dodds, Rod Barry, Peter Websdello, Simon Powell, Mike Swanson, Adam Perry, Nici Riley, Louise Sutcliffe, Ms Heulwen, Kate Arkless Gray, Andrew Purvis, Don Turnbull, Penny Markell, Gemma Ward, Vicky Dean, Anna Campbell, Bernie Caffarey, Rob Townsend, Adrian Thompson, Joe, Emma Worby, Eugenia Barrajo Serra, Lee Bennett, Richard Poynton, and everyone else in Join Me...